Conversation Starters

for

JojoMoyes's

The Girl You Left Behind

By dailyBooks

FREE Download: Get the Hottest Books!
*Get Your Free Books with **_Any Purchase_** of* Conversation Starters!

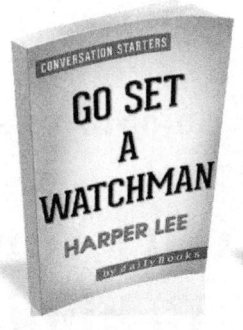

Every purchase comes with a FREE download of the hottest titles!

Add spice to any conversation
Never run out of things to say
Spend time with those you love

Read it for FREE on any smartphone, tablet, Kindle, PC or Mac.
No purchase necessary - licensed for personal enjoyment only.

Get it Now

or Click Here.

Scan Your Phone

Please Note: This is an unofficial conversation starters guide. If you have not yet read the original work, please do so first.

**Copyright © 2015 by dailyBooks. All Rights Reserved.
First Published in the United States of America 2015**

We hope you enjoy this complementary guide from **dailyBooks.** *We aim to provide quality, thought provoking material to assistin your discovery and discussions on some of today's favorite books.*

Disclaimer / Terms of Use: Product names, logos, brands, and other trademarks featured or referred to within this publication are the property of their respective trademark holders and are not affiliated with dailyBooks. The publisher and author make no representations or warranties with respect to the accuracy or completeness of these contents and disclaim all warranties such as warranties of fitness for a particular purpose. This guide is unofficial and unauthorized. It is not authorized, approved, licensed, or endorsed by the original book's author or publisher and any of their licensees or affiliates.

No part of this publication may be reproduced or retransmitted, electronic or mechanical, without the written permission of the publisher.

Tips for Using dailyBooks Conversation Starters:

EVERY GOOD BOOK CONTAINS A WORLD FAR DEEPER THAN the surface of its pages. The characters and their world come alive through the words on the pages, yet the characters and its world still live on. Questions herein are designed to bring us beneath the surface of the page and invite us into the world that lives on. These questions can be used to:

- Foster a deeper understanding of the book
- Promote an atmosphere of discussion for groups
- Assist in the study of the book, either individually or corporately
- Explore unseen realms of the book as never seen before

About Us:

THROUGH YEARS OF EXPERIENCE AND FIELD EXPERTISE, from newspaper featured book clubs to local library chapters, *dailyBooks* can bring your book discussion to life. Host your book party as we discuss some of today's most widely read books.

Table of Contents

Introducing *The Girl You Left Behind*
Introducing the Author

question 1
question 2
question 3
question 4
question 5
question 6
question 7
question 8
question 9
question 10
question 11
question12
question 13
question 14
question 15
question 16
question 17
question 18
question 19
question 20
question21
question22
question 23
question 24
question 25
question 26
question 27
question 28
question 29
question 30
question 31
question32

question 33
question 34
question 35
question 36
question 37
question 38
question 39
question 40
question 41
question 42
question 43
question 44
question 45
question 46
question 47
question 48
question 49
question 50

Introducing *The Girl You Left Behind*

AFTER SOPHIE RELUCTANTLY MODELS FOR FAMOUS ARTIST EdouardLefevre, they fall madly in love. Unfortunately, their time together is shortened when World War I breaks out, and Edouard enlists in the French army. Sophie is left behind in the French village of St. Peronne. Sophie and her sister Helene share in their fear as they both await the return of their husbands. Together they take care of their brother as well as Helene's two children. They are also left to run Le Coq Rouge, their family's hotel.

Eventually, the Germans take over the hotel, and things begin to look bleak for the families of this small French village. When a German Kommandant arrives that reveals an appreciation for art, especially the painting of Sophie, a dangerous obsession begins to grow that will force Sophie into a deal that she thinks will saveEdouard's life. Her relationship with the Kommandant threatens the friends and family that Sophie has worked so hard to protect.

The book moves forward a century where we find Sophie's portrait hanging on the wall in Liv's house. Liv is a young widow, still grieving the loss of her husband, David. He was a renowned architect and designed the beautiful glass house Liv still lives in, even though she can hardly afford it. David purchased the portrait for Liv while on their honeymoon, and Liv cherishes it more than anything now that her husband is gone.

Although devastated by the loss of David, Liv sees a glimmer of hope when she meets Paul, who works for an organization called TARP, which works to recover stolen art. Paul's next case is none other than *The Girl You Left Behind,* a paintingby EdouardLefevre whose artwork has recently become increasingly popular. While Edouard's family is formulating a case to recover the artwork, Liv begins researching the story behind the portrait as well as Sophie's story.

The Girl You Left Behind focuses not only on the love stories of Sophie and Liv but also on the case to find out who the rightful owner of the portrait is. Just how far will Liv go to preserve her possession of the painting?

Introducing the Author

NEW YORK TIMES BESTSELLING AUTHOR, JOJO MOYES, WAS born and raised in London, England. Her given name was Pauline Sara Jo Moyes, but she is known as JojoMoyes, her pen name. Moyes attended Royal Holloway and Bedford New College in London. *The Independent* financed a bursary for her to attend City University to study newspaper journalism.

Moyes has worked various jobs over the years, including Brailletypist and brochure writer. She also worked as a journalist for the *South China Morning Post* and *The Independent.* She published her first book, *Sheltering Rain,* in 2002 and has since been a full-time novelist and journalist. Other than her published novels, you can find her work published in *The Daily Telegraph.*

Moyes has written twelve novels that have been published in eleven languages worldwide. Her most popular work includes*Honeymoon in Paris, Silver Bay, The Last Letter from Your Lover, One Plus One, The Girl You Left Behind,* and *Me Before You.* She won the Romantic Novel of the Year Award two times for *Foreign Fruit* in 2004 and in 2001 for *The Last Letter from Your Lover*. The award is given by the Romantic Novelists' Association in the UK. She was also nominated for Book of the Year for *Me Before You,* which has sold over three million copies.

Moyes prefers to write without distraction and often confines herself to small places to focus on her writing. She often gets her inspiration from news stories that she reads and tends to focus on the "gray area" of those stories, which are usually somewhat controversial topics, including *Me Before You,* which is her favorite book that she has written so far.

Moyes currently resides in Essex with her husband and three children. Her husband, Charles Arthur, is also a journalist.

Discussion Questions

question 1

EdouardLefevre was an artist in the early 1900s in France. In the portrait he painted of his wife, do you think he was trying to depict who she was then or who he thought she could be? Explain your answer.

question 2

Hoping that the Kommandant would reunite her with Edouard, Sophie made a risky deal with him. Do you think Edouard would have appreciated her sacrifice? Why or why not?

question 3

Aurelien did not approve of Sophie's relationship with the Kommandant, and he reacted very angrily. What do you think made him react in this way?

. . . .

question 4

The Kommandment became obsessed with the painting and Liv. Did you ever feel any sympathy for the Kammandant? What do you think Liv's true feelings toward the Kommandant were?

. . . .

question 5

Liliane was a member of the French resistance. How did you feel about the way the villagers treated her? Did your opinion change after you learned the truth?

question 6

Sophie and Liv, the two main characters in the book, seem to both be unfairly judged by society. Why do you think the author wanted them to be judged in this way? In what ways did this contribute to the storyline?

question 7

Liv feels very strongly about the portrait of Sophie, so strongly, in fact, that she believes she cannot live without it and is ready to risk losing her home for it. Explain why she was so enamored by the painting. Can you think of any material thing in your life for which you would be willing to fight so hard?

question 8

Paul was afraid that Liv would resent him for losing the painting. Do you think his feelings were justified? Why or why not?

question 9

The story is a dual narrative telling the stories of Sophie and Liv. Did you enjoy this style of writing, or did it make for a difficult to follow storyline? Did you feel more of a connection to Sophie's or Liv's story?

question 10

The title of the book is *The Girl You Left Behind*. Do you think the title refers to just the name of the painting, or did it refer to something else? Explain your answer.

question 11

Fran, a homeless woman, lived in Liv's building. What effect does Liv and Fran's relationship have on Liv's life?

question 12

Liv still lives in the glass house that her husband designed. What do you think the glass house symbolizes in the story?

question 13

Although the stories in the book are fictional, the author conducted a lot of research to make her story as historically accurate as possible. Do you think she was able to tell the two women's stories and maintain historical accuracy? Explain your answer.

question 14

The author presents Sophie's story in the first person, which gives the reader a more intimate look into the life of the narrator. In what ways did this perspective help you to empathize better with Sophie?

question 15

In the book, the interest in Lefevre's work is growing, and the painting is becoming very valuable in terms of money. When Liv's husband died, she found herself suffering financially. Do you the monetary value of the painting had any effect on Liv's desire to keep the painting? Explain why you feel this way.

question 16

A reviewer for *Entertainment Weekly* said that JojoMoyes took "careful interest in the dark corners" that are present in love stories. What do you think the reviewer meant by dark corners?

question 17

Having a 4.5-star average review on Amazon, a majority of the readers of this book gave it high praises. Do you agree with the majority? What would you have rated the book and why?

question 18

A reviewer for *Parade* magazine said that the author did a good job of weaving Sophie's and Liv's stories. Do you agree with this review? What were some of the ways that JojoMoyes connected the two stories?

question 19

One reviewer said that Sophie's story was much more emotional and a more enjoyable read than Liv's story. Do you agree with this reviewer? Which story did you enjoy most, Sophie's or Liv's? Why?

question 20

One reviewer said that the beginning of Liv's story fell flat but eventually piqued her interest. How do you think the author could have made the transition from Sophie's story to Liv's story more interesting?

FREE Download: Get the Hottest Books!
*Get Your Free Books with **Any Purchase** of Conversation Starters!*

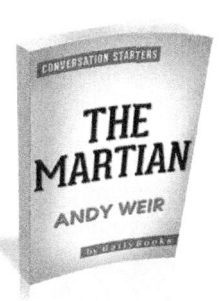

Every purchase comes with a FREE download of the hottest titles!

Add spice to any conversation
Never run out of things to say
Spend time with those you love

Read it for FREE on any smartphone, tablet, Kindle, PC or Mac.
No purchase necessary - licensed for personal enjoyment only.

Get it Now

or Click Here.

Scan Your Phone

question 21

One reviewer said that the author did a great job with the description and storyline that took place during World War I. Historically speaking, do you think the author did a good job depicting life during the war? Why or why not?

question 22

Many readers said they found the story during the war to be educational and enlightening. What did you learn from this book about living in times of war?

question 23

The book has been called a historical fiction, and a few reviewers have commented that the author helped them understand what it would have been like to have a husband away at war in WWI. Did you have this same emotional experience while reading the book? Describe how these emotions affected you.

question 24

A few reviewers commented that they did not like Liv's character because her attachment to the painting was "ridiculous" and "unrealistic." Do you agree with this judgment of her character? Why or why not?

question 25

Many readers bought *The Girl You Left Behind* simply because of the success of *Me Before You,* also written by JojoMoyes. If you did the same, were you disappointed in this book? Which book do you think was better and why?

question 26

JojoMoyes was born Pauline Sara Jo Moyes. Why do you think she chose a pen name to write under?

question 27

Moyes has stated that she gets many of the ideas for her stories from news stories. How do you think her work as a journalist has played into this inspiration preference?

question 28

Moyes has won the Romantic Novel of the Year Award twice. Do you think her work is deserving of such an award? Why or why not?

question 29

Moyes seems to write about controversial topics in her novels. Do you think this is why so many are drawn to her work? Explain.

question 30

Moyes says she wrote *The Girl You Left Behind* because she knew very little about France during World War I. Do you think the book shed new light on this topic for her readers? Tell something you learned about that period that you did not know before you read this book.

question 31

Sophie made a deal with the Kommandant with the hope that he would reunite her with Edouard. Would you have made the same or similar deal? Why or why not?

. . . .

question 32

Many of the people in St. Peronne dealt with extreme hunger. If you were in the same position, how far would you have been willing to go to feed yourself and your family?

. . . .

question 33

Although Liv's husband acquired the portrait legally, Edouard's family was the rightful owner of the portrait. If you were Liv, would you have fought for the portrait, even after learning the truth?

question 34

Liv was willing to save the portrait rather than her home. Would you have done the same thing if you were in her position? Why or why not?

question 35

Sophie and her sister Helene were not only forced to take care of the children and home, but it was also necessary for them to run the family's hotel after their husbands went away to fight in the war. This was not an uncommon occurrence. Although it is not the main theme of this book, do you think the war played a role in advancing the cause of women's rights in the world? Would you have had the courage to do the same if you were in their position? Why or why not?

question 36

Liv's husband died suddenly at a young age, which left Liv financially and emotionally devastated. Do you think Liv would have been so attached to the painting if her husband had not passed away?

question 37

In recent years, Edouard's painting became increasingly popular, which increased the value of his work. If this was not the case and the painting had minimal value, do you think Edouard's family would have fought so hard for the painting?

question 38

Liv's story was told in the third person. How would the story have been different if it were told from her perspective (first person)?

Quiz Questions

question39

True or False: Sophie was married to Edouard when he painted her portrait.

question40

Edouard went away to fight in _____.

question41

Sophie and her sister Helene take on the responsibility of running the family hotel called _____.

question42

True or False: The French army takes over the family hotel?

question 43

Liv's house is made of _____.

question 44

True or False: Liv meets Paul during his investigation of her portrait.

question 45

Paul works for an organization called _____.

question 46

JojoMoyes was born and raised in _____.

question 47

True or False: JojoMoyes worked as a Braille typist before becoming a novelist.

question 48

True or False: JojoMoyes first published book was *Me Before You*.

question 49

JojoMoyes currently lives on a farm in _____.

question 50

The inspiration for most of JojoMoyes books comes from
_____.

QuizAnswers

1. False; they had just met
2. World War I
3. Le Coq Rouge
4. False; the Germans take over the hotel
5. glass
6. TARP
7. False; they met prior to the investigation
8. London
9. True
10. False; her first published book was Sheltering Rain
11. Essex
12. news stories

THE END

Want to promote your book group? Register here.

PLEASE LEAVE US A FEEDBACK.

THANK YOU!

FREE Download: Get the Hottest Books!
*Get Your Free Books with **Any Purchase** of* Conversation Starters!

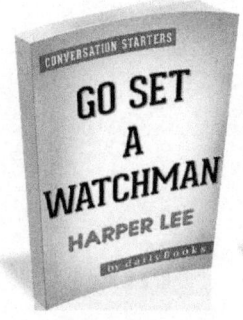

Every purchase comes with a FREE download of the hottest titles!

Add spice to any conversation
Never run out of things to say
Spend time with those you love

Read it for FREE on any smartphone, tablet, Kindle, PC or Mac.
No purchase necessary - licensed for personal enjoyment only.

Get it Now

or Click Here.

Scan Your Phone

Printed in Great Britain
by Amazon